PAKISTAN
in Pictures

Stacy Taus-Bolstad

Lerner Publications Company

Contents

Lerner Publishing Group realizes that current information and statistics quickly become out of date. To extend the usefulness of the Visual Geography Series, we developed www.vgsbooks.com, a website offering links to up-to-date information, as well as in-depth material, on a wide variety of subjects. All of the websites listed on www.vgsbooks.com have been carefully selected by researchers at Lerner Publishing Group. However, Lerner Publishing Group is not responsible for the accuracy or suitability of the material on any website other than <www.lernerbooks.com>. It is recommended that students using the Internet be supervised by a parent or teacher. Links on www.vgsbooks.com will be regularly reviewed and updated as needed.

Website address: www.lernerbooks.com

Lerner Publications Company
A division of Lerner Publishing Group
241 First Avenue North
Minneapolis, MN 55401 U.S.A.

web enhanced @ www.vgsbooks.com

Library of Congress Cataloging-in-Publication Data

Taus-Bolstad, Stacy.
    Pakistan in pictures / by Stacy Taus-Bolstad.– Rev. and expanded ed.
      p. cm. – (Visual geography series)
    Summary: Describes the geography, history, government, economy, people,and cultural life of
Pakistan. Includes bibliographical references and index.
    ISBN: 0-8225-4682-5 (lib. bdg. : alk. paper)
    1. Pakistan. 2. Pakistan—Pictorial works. [1. Pakistan.] I. Title. II. Visual geography series
[Minneapolis, Minn.]
DS376.9 .T36 2003
954.9–dc21   2002008575

Manufactured in the United States of America
1 2 3 4 5 6 – JR – 08 07 06 05 04 03

INTRODUCTION

The Islamic Republic of Pakistan stepped into the spotlight at the dawn of the twenty-first century when it become a key player in an international war on terrorism. This campaign was launched by the United States after terrorist attacks killed thousands of people in New York City and Washington, D.C., on September 11, 2001. These attacks were believed to have been conceived and carried out by members of al-Qaeda, an informal international network of Islamic terrorist groups. At the time of the attacks, the groups' leader, Osama bin Laden, was based in Afghanistan, Pakistan's neighbor and long-time ally. In exchange for economic aid, Pakistan agreed to provide intelligence, border control measures, and military assistance to the United States. In so doing, Pakistan faces the challenge of balancing its cooperation with the international campaign against terrorism with the interests of its Islamic population. This crisis will directly impact the country's economic and political development in the years to come.

Conflict is not new to Pakistan. The country emerged as an independent nation in 1947, following centuries of religious and ethnic conflict in the region. Located in south central Asia, Pakistan shares a long, sometimes bitter history with its eastern neighbor India.

Pakistan's history dates back to ancient civilizations that emerged around 2500 B.C. Over the centuries, various empires rose to power, bringing with them religious and cultural changes that would shape the beliefs and customs of modern Pakistan. Among the most influential of these was the religion of Islam, introduced to the region by merchants from the Arabian Peninsula in the seventh century A.D. Since then, Islam has served as a unifying force among Pakistan's diverse ethnic groups, which include the Punjabis, the Sindhi, the Pathan, and the Baluchi. Beginning in the 1500s, the Mughal Empire also left its mark on Pakistan. Britain took control of parts of Pakistan in the 1700s.

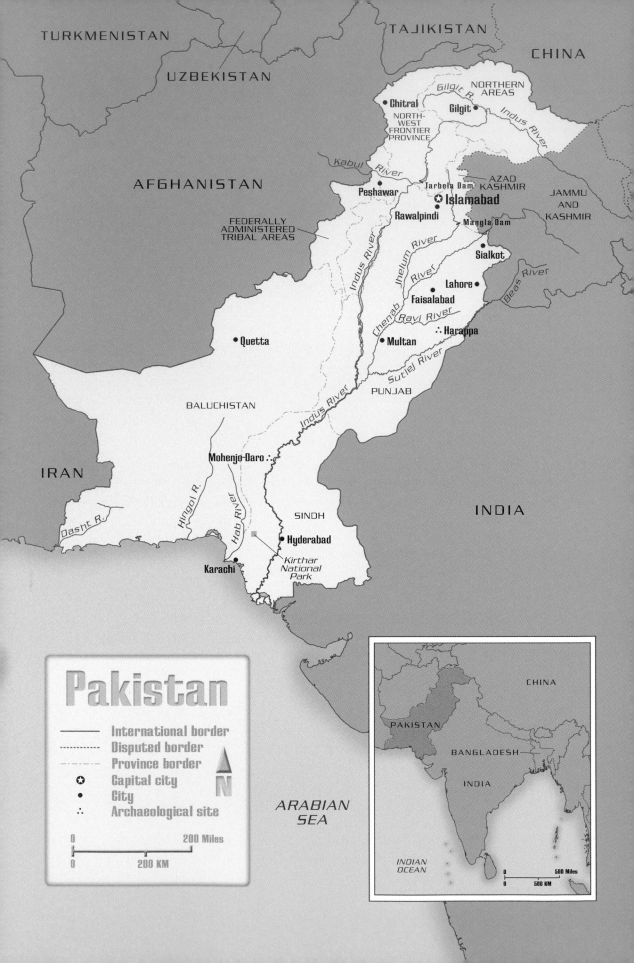

By the early twentieth century, Muslims (followers of Islam) living in British-ruled India began to demand an independent nation, called Pakistan, for themselves. These Muslims believed that India's Hindu religious majority exercised too much influence over Islamic cultural, political, and economic life.

In August 1947, Pakistan became a reality. The new nation was made up of two Muslim-dominated territories—West Pakistan and East Pakistan—separated by more than 1,000 miles (1,609 kilometers) of Indian territory.

Since independence, Pakistan has faced many conflicts. For example, civil war broke out in 1971 between West Pakistan and East Pakistan, resulting in the latter becoming the independent nation of Bangladesh. In addition, Pakistan and India are locked in an ongoing conflict over control of Jammu and Kashmir, a region located along Pakistan's northeastern border with India. Complicating matters, martial law and military leaders have dominated more than half of Pakistan's history as a self-governing nation. In recent years, Pakistan's largest province, Baluchistan, has struggled with ethnic and nationalist conflicts. In addition, a rising growth rate continues to tax Pakistan's natural resources.

Pakistan's leadership has yet to mold the nation's diverse ethnic communities into a unified nation in which Islam and democracy can coexist. Finding a national identity that satisfies all of the country's ethnic groups and balancing its internal and international priorities remain significant challenges for Pakistan.

JAMMU AND KASHMIR

At the heart of the dispute over Jammu and Kashmir lies a controversial document called the Instrument of Accession. According to this document, the Hindu Maharaja of Kashmir signed the area over to India in 1947, though Kashmir had a Muslim majority population. The people of Kashmir and the government of Pakistan do not accept India's claim and even question the existence of the document.

THE LAND

Pakistan covers the northwestern portion of the Indian subcontinent, a region in southern Asia. With more than 300,000 square miles (777,000 square kilometers) of territory, Pakistan is slightly larger than the state of Texas.

The Arabian Sea forms Pakistan's southern boundary, Iran lies to the southwest, and Afghanistan is located to the west and northwest. China lies to the northeast, and India stretches along Pakistan's eastern frontier. India and Pakistan disagree about their mutual boundary in Jammu and Kashmir. The Simla Accord of 1972 stabilized a cease-fire line and gave each of the two nations a section of the disputed land.

◉ Topography

The Islamic Republic of Pakistan has three main landscape features. A mountainous region, which is interrupted by deep gorges and narrow passages, is situated along the nation's northern frontier. The Indus

River divides the southern portion of the nation into two regions: the Indus River Valley in the west and the Baluchistan Plateau in the east.

Pakistan's rugged mountain region has long been difficult to travel through and to settle. A chain of mountains called the Hindu Kush rises in northern Pakistan. The range's highest peak is Tirich Mir, at 25,230 feet (7,690 meters) above sea level.

The Hindu Kush blends into the Karakoram Range, which Pakistan and India share in the disputed territory of Jammu and Kashmir. This range has about sixty peaks, the tallest of which is K2, also called Godwin Austen, at 28,250 feet (8,610 m). This peak lies in Pakistan's section of the territory.

Just south of the Hindu Kush and Karakoram Range is a small section of the Himalaya Mountains, a range that stretches for 1,500 miles (2,414 km) along the northern edge of the Indian subcontinent. At 26,600 feet (8,108 m), Nanga Parbat is the tallest mountain in Pakistan's portion of the Himalayas.

A KILLER MOUNTAIN

At more than 28,000 feet (8,534 m) above sea level, Pakistan's K2 is the second highest mountain in the world. It is also considered the most dangerous to climb. In 1902 the first organized mountain-climbing expedition attempted K2. By the 1950s, five separate mountain-climbing expeditions had tried and failed to reach the summit. Several climbers lost their lives during these attempts.

K2 remained unconquered until August 31, 1954, when an Italian team successfully scaled the peak. In 1986 nine different expeditions climbed K2, and seven climbers reached the top. Despite their success, K2 claimed the lives of thirteen people that same year.

Passes, or gaps, in these mountain chains provide access through the rugged terrain to neighboring countries. The Khyber Pass, located west of the city of Peshawar, provides a route through the Safed Koh Range to Afghanistan. Similarly, the Baroghil, Khunjrab, and Karakoram Passes connect Pakistan to northern Afghanistan and China.

The Indus River divides southern Pakistan into two neighboring sections. The Indus River Valley, which lies east of the waterway, covers the provinces of Sindh and Punjab and stretches into western India. The Indus has deposited tons of rich soil in the region, making it a fertile agricultural area about 100 miles (161 km) long and 150 miles (241 km) wide. In addition, secondary rivers flow into the Indus, providing further sources of water for crops.

The southeastern portion of the Indus region gradually becomes drier until it blends into the Thar Desert,

A highway winds through the Khyber Pass in the Safed Koh Range. Travelers use the pass to make their way between Pakistan and Afghanistan.

Terraced fields line the banks of the Indus River, which cuts through an otherwise arid Pakistan. The Indus is a source of water for much of the country's farmland.

which lies mostly in western India. The Indus River's delta—a triangular, silt-laden region where the river spreads into several outlets (mouths) to the sea—appears just southeast of Karachi, the nation's chief port.

The region to the west of the Indus lies mostly in the province of Baluchistan. Dry and sparsely vegetated, the Baluchistan Plateau contains a number of low mountain ranges. The Toba Kakar Range curves along Pakistan's western border, with Khojak Pass providing access to Afghanistan. Along the Indus River is the Sulaiman Range, whose highest peaks rise 11,000 feet (3,353 m) above sea level.

The Siahan and Kirthar Ranges fan outward to the southwest and south, respectively, reaching heights of more than 6,000 feet (1,829 m) and 7,000 feet (2,134 m). On the Baluchistan Plateau, particularly near the city of Quetta, earthquake tremors occur frequently, although the last massive disturbance was in 1935.

◉ Rivers

Of Pakistan's rivers, the Indus is by far the most important. Intensive farming is possible in eastern sections of the country because the Indus and other rivers irrigate the region.

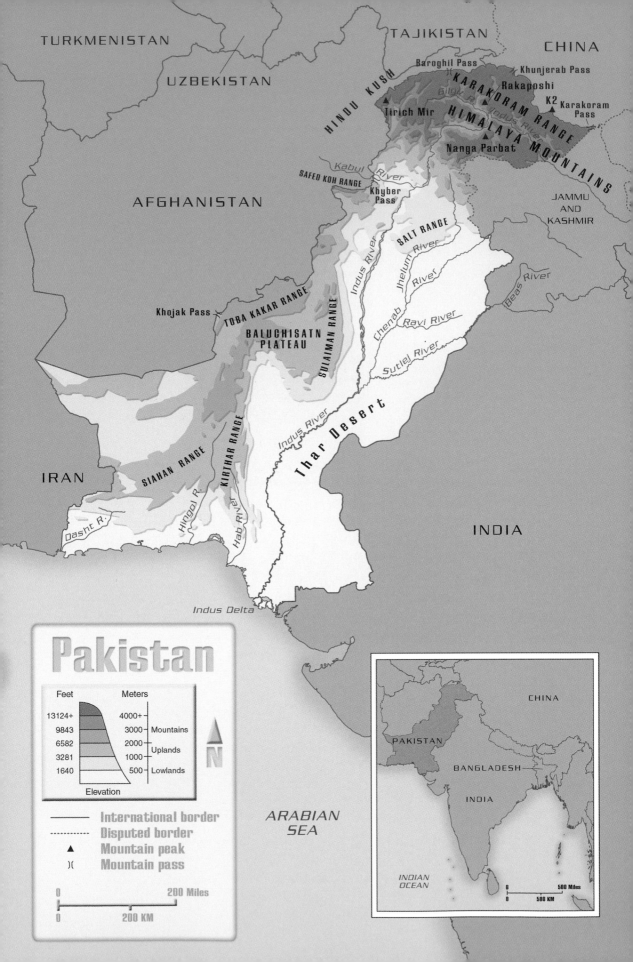

TURKMENISTAN

UZBEKISTAN

TAJIKISTAN

CHINA

Baroghil Pass

Khunjerab Pass

HINDU KUSH

KARAKORAM RANGE

Rakaposhi

K2

Karakoram
Pass

Tirich Mir

HIMALAYA MOUNTAINS

Gilgit R.

Indus River

AFGHANISTAN

Nanga Parbat

Kabul
River

JAMMU
AND
KASHMIR

SAFED KOH RANGE

Khyber
Pass

SALT RANGE

Jhelum River

Indus River

Chenab

Ravi River

Beas River

KHOJAK PASS

TOBA KAKAR RANGE

SULAIMAN RANGE

BALUCHISATN
PLATEAU

Sutlej River

Khojak Pass

SIAHAN RANGE

KIRTHAR RANGE

Hingol R.

Hab River

Indus River

Thar Desert

INDIA

Dasht R.

IRAN

Indus Delta

Pakistan

Feet	Meters	
13124+	4000+	
9843	3000	Mountains
6582	2000	Uplands
3281	1000	
1640	500	Lowlands

Elevation

N

—— International border
------ Disputed border
▲ Mountain peak
)(Mountain pass

0   200 Miles
0   200 KM

ARABIAN
SEA

CHINA

PAKISTAN

BANGLADESH

INDIA

INDIAN
OCEAN

0   500 Miles
0   500 KM

An irrigation canal in Baluchistan provides water for the area's farmland.

The Indus River rises near Mount Kailas in Tibet, flows westward into Pakistan, and turns southward in the northern highlands. Its 1,800-mile-long (2,897-km) course leads to the Arabian Sea. Small steamers can navigate the Indus as far as the city of Hyderabad. The river also powers hydroelectric facilities at Tarbela Dam in the North-West Frontier Province (NWFP).

Several secondary rivers—the Jhelum, the Chenab, the Ravi, the Beas, and the Sutlej—travel through Pakistan and eventually join the Indus River. Together they empty into the Arabian Sea through the Indus delta. More than half of the total land under cultivation in Pakistan depends on a vast system of irrigation canals that draws water from the Indus and its contributing rivers.

The Gilgit River, a northern tributary of the Indus, travels about 150 miles (241 km) through the administrative district called the Northern Areas. The Kabul River begins in Afghanistan and flows eastward into the Indus. Although generally dry, the Baluchistan Plateau has several small waterways—including the Dasht, the Hingol, and the Hab Rivers—that empty into the Arabian Sea.

◎ Climate

Temperatures in the northern mountains average about 75°F (24°C) in summer (mid-April to mid-July) and drop below freezing in winter (November to January). Summer is considerably hotter in the Indus region, with temperatures that can rise to 110°F (43°C). The sea breezes that cool coastal Karachi most of the year turn hot and dusty in the summer, but the climate generally ranges between 66°F (19°C) and 86°F (30°C). Temperatures in Baluchistan average about 80°F (27°C) in summer and 40°F (4°C) in winter.

Most of Pakistan's rainfall occurs between July and September, when a seasonal wind, called a monsoon, blows across the country. Pakistan averages only 10 inches (25 centimeters) of precipitation each year, with Punjab receiving the largest share—up to 20 inches (51 cm) in a year. Southern areas of the Baluchistan Plateau get the least rainfall, usually less than 5 inches (13 cm) per year. Despite these general patterns, rainfall can vary greatly from year to year, and Pakistan has experienced both floods and droughts.

Flora and Fauna

Pakistan's plant life varies according to altitude, with higher elevations supporting hardy vegetation such as firs, pines, junipers, and Himalayan chinars (a Eurasian shade tree). Flowers in the mountains include wild roses and edelweiss, a year-round herb that flourishes at high altitudes.

Cosmos bloom in a mountain valley. The snow-covered peak in the background is Rakaposhi Mountain, which rises near the town of Gilgit in northern Pakistan.

The Indus region—the scene of much of Pakistan's agricultural activity—has fruit-bearing trees such as mangoes, guavas, and bananas. Cereal grains thrive in the fertile soil, as do walnut trees, grapevines, and berry bushes. Jasmine, Pakistan's national flower, thrives in this part of the country. In dry and desert regions, sparse grasses or stunted vegetation are most common, although date palms sometimes appear.

Hawks and eagles inhabit the northern mountain zone, where unusual mammals include the snow leopard, the Marco Polo sheep, and the Himalayan black bear. Several varieties of wild goats—such as the markhor and the ibex—also live in the rugged terrain.

The plains support herds of deer, goats, sheep, and water buffalo, and the desert regions are home to jackals, hyenas, and camels. Along the coast, the most

The markhor, a member of the goat family, is Pakistan's national animal. Markhors can grow to weigh almost 250 pounds (113 kilograms). They have large horns that either grow straight or flare out, depending on the subspecies. Markhors live in sparsely wooded mountainous areas and graze on grass or leaves. Some even climb trees to munch leaves and twigs. The markhors' horns have made them valuable hunting trophies. Overhunting and loss of habitat threaten the markhor population.

This young markhor is among the few species of animals that live in the steep, chilly mountains of northern Pakistan.

common forms of wildlife are the fish and reptiles that inhabit the Arabian Sea and the delta of the Indus River. Herring, mackerel, and sharks live in the sea, and crocodiles thrive in the delta's marshy areas.

Visit vgsbooks.com for links to websites where you can find photographs and information on Pakistan's cities, landscapes, and wildlife—including the markhor goat. You can also find up-to-date population figures, current weather conditions, and more.

Natural Resources

Pakistan has a variety of mineral resources, but the country uses very few of these. Lack of capital, technology, and transportation systems have all hampered the growth of Pakistan's mining industry. Government-sponsored studies and several private companies are working to upgrade the country's mineral production.

While searching for oil, scientists discovered large reserves of natural gas in Baluchistan. The gas is used for fuel, fertilizer, and petrochemicals. Low-grade coal deposits are also mined, but production satisfies less than 6 percent of Pakistan's commercial energy requirements.

Deposits of chromite (used to make chrome) and bauxite (the raw material for aluminum) exist in Pakistan, and significant deposits of copper, iron ore, manganese, sulfur, gold, and graphite have also been discovered. These minerals are difficult to reach, however, because of their location in Baluchistan, where ethnic and nationalist conflicts have occurred in recent times.

The fast growth rate of Pakistan's population has also caused problems for the country's natural resources. Deforestation has contributed to agricultural runoff and soil erosion. Industrial waste and motor vehicle exhaust pollute the country's air and water.

In 1992 the government released a National Conservation Strategy Report addressing the problems of Pakistan's environment. To reduce pollution, the government issued stricter regulations in 1993 for factories, cities, and motor vehicles. Lack of funding makes these laws hard to enforce, however, and by the late 1990s only 3 percent of Pakistan's industries had complied with the new regulations.

Cities

Established in 1961, the capital city of Islamabad (population 792,000) lies at the foothills of the Himalayas in northern Pakistan. A carefully planned urban center, Islamabad blends modern and traditional architectural styles and has distinct governmental, business, and residential zones.

Modern government and office buildings dot the **skyline of Islamabad.**

Buses and people clog the streets of Karachi, Pakistan's most populated city.

Although most Pakistanis still live in rural villages, the population of major cities has increased steadily since the 1970s. Karachi, with a population of more than nine million, is Pakistan's largest city and the capital of Sindh province. The city served as the nation's first capital, from 1947 to 1959. Once a small fishing village on the Arabian Sea, the city features many modern buildings and is an important commercial and financial hub.

Karachi is also the home of factories that manufacture chemicals, textiles, and glassware, and it is a shipping outlet for Pakistan's foreign trade. As the country's largest city and commercial center, Karachi faces problems such as ethnic and political tensions, overcrowding, and pollution.

About 650 miles (1,046 km) northeast of Karachi is Lahore, Pakistan's second largest city, with a population of about five million. Lahore is the nation's cultural center and the capital of Punjab. Records of a settlement at Lahore date back more than one thousand years, and the city was an important site for Mughal and British administrations. Among the most important remains of the Mughal era are the Shalimar Gardens, which the Mughal emperor Shah Jahan designed in 1642.

Also in Punjab is Rawalpindi (population 1.4 million). Once the headquarters of regional British administrators, Rawalpindi served as a temporary capital until the current capital, Islamabad, was built.

A horse-drawn cart passes through the narrow streets of **Lahore's old city.**

The capital of the North-West Frontier Province, Peshawar (population 988,000) lies near the entrance to the Khyber Pass. As a result, its largely Pathan (also known as Pashtun) ethnic population grew during the 1970s and 1980s when thousands of Afghan refugees fled conflict in their homeland. Because of an agreement made with the United States after the September 11, 2001, attacks, Pakistan closed its borders to Afghan refugees, although some managed to cross the border to escape the air and ground strikes waged by U.S. forces. An estimated two million Afghans live in Pakistan.

Because of its strategic location, Peshawar was long used as a frontier settlement for Asian trade caravans. In modern times, the city manufactures footwear and textiles, processes locally grown food, and trades handicrafts.

HISTORY AND GOVERNMENT

Archaeological findings, including cave paintings and stone tools, indicate that humans probably settled on the Indian subcontinent 400,000 years ago. Large-scale settlements in Pakistan began about 2500 B.C., along the fertile banks of the Indus River and its many tributaries. A complex urban civilization grew in this region and, at its peak, included western India.

◉ Early Empires

Archaeologists have uncovered about four hundred prehistoric cities on the Indian subcontinent and around Pakistan. This civilization, known as the Indus civilization, had cities with extensive drainage systems and well-defined neighborhoods. A system of picture writing existed, but modern experts have yet to decipher it.

The two main urban centers of this ancient civilization were Mohenjo-Daro, in what is modern-day Sindh, and Harappa, in present-day Punjab. Mohenjo-Daro had wide streets that were sometimes paved. Buildings here included public administration centers, religious colleges, and royal palaces.

Harappa, the first of the Indus cities to be discovered, is smaller and less preserved than Mohenjo-Daro. The economy of Harappa depended on trade and farming, and its buildings included a fortress.

The Indus civilization ended around 1700 B.C. Aryans, people from central Asia, conquered northern regions of the subcontinent between 2000 and 1000 B.C. The Aryans developed a philosophy that evolved into the Hindu religion. Their social framework included a caste system, under which citizens became members of rigid social and professional groups. The Aryans also introduced iron tools, the horse and chariot, and astronomy and mathematics to the region.

Sixteen political units arose in the Aryans' territory over the next one thousand years. Their realm stretched across the northern subcontinent from modern Afghanistan to Bangladesh. By about the middle of the sixth century B.C., Magadha had emerged as the most

Alexander the Great was a Greek leader who conquered part of the area that would eventually become Pakistan.

powerful of these states. Magadha's location in northeastern India, as well as its access to rich soil and iron deposits, helped make it a stable kingdom. Magadha's rise was accompanied by religious reform movements that resulted in the founding of Buddhism and Jainism, religious offshoots of Hinduism.

At roughly the same time as Magadha's rise to power, northern Pakistan came under the authority of the Gandhara kingdom, which was centered near present-day Peshawar. In 522 B.C., the empire of Persia (modern-day Iran) captured Punjab and Sindh. The small region remained part of the Persian Empire for more than two hundred years.

Greek ruler Alexander the Great took control of the Persian Empire in 330 B.C., and in 326 B.C. he entered Punjab. Although Alexander managed to capture chunks of Punjab, his travel-weary army soon tired of the wars and rebelled, forcing Alexander to return to Greece.

The Magadha leader Chandragupta Maurya conquered Gandhara shortly after Alexander's departure. By 321 B.C., he had founded the Mauryan Empire, which governed all of Pakistan and much of India for about a century. The most famous of the Maurya rulers was Chandragupta's grandson Asoka, who reigned from 273 to 232 B.C. Buddhism became the official religion of Asoka's realm, and he encouraged the construction of many massive Buddhist buildings. But Asoka's empire did not survive long after his death in 232 B.C., and within a century the empire shrank to the original borders of Magadha.

After the Mauryan Empire disintegrated, Gandhara flourished as a cultural center within the Kushan Empire. The Kushan, who came from the Hindu Kush, developed Perushapure (near Peshawar) as their capital and ruled between A.D. 50 and about A.D. 250. Their territory included areas of modern Afghanistan, China, the former Soviet Union, Pakistan, and India.

Kushan's economy depended on peaceful trade. By the first century A.D., the Kushan controlled sections of caravan routes, including the Silk Road, which linked the Persian, Chinese, and Roman Empires.

In the fourth century, the Gupta Empire in eastern India absorbed the area that became Pakistan. The Guptas followed Hinduism and made discoveries in mathematics, astronomy, and the arts. Scholars compiled dictionaries of the Sanskrit language, which was used at the time, and mathematicians calculated the shape and movement of the planets.

By the seventh century, Hindu and Buddhist dynasties throughout the subcontinent were competing for former Gupta territory. Many of these rivals were based in Punjab and belonged to the Rajput clan, whose soldiers were famous for their military skills.

The Gupta Empire was one of peace and prosperity, and Gupta leaders encouraged scientific and artistic pursuits. During this era, Gupta mathematicians developed the concept of zero and the decimal system based on the number ten. Physicians made strides in plastic surgery and even vaccinated against diseases such as smallpox.

This illustration depicts the Rajput style of dress. The Rajput clan was known for its military might.

At the same time, a new religion, Islam, was founded in the seventh century by the prophet Muhammad in what eventually became Saudi Arabia. This religion would soon become a driving force in the area around the former Gupta Empire.

Muslim Rule and the Mughal Empire

Muslims—followers of Islam—were urged to spread their beliefs by expanding their territory and converting conquered peoples to Islam. Muslim sailors from Arabia first arrived in the area shortly after Muhammad's death in A.D. 632. Muslim traders also conducted business along the coast of the Arabian Sea, bringing their new faith with them.

In the Punjab and Sindh regions of Pakistan, people welcomed Islam. Many Hindus at the bottom of the caste system converted to Islam because it did not include social divisions. Islamic Turks and Afghans, who had moved from the west and who had settled in Pakistan and India, also helped to spread Islam.

Muslim attacks on Pakistan began in earnest under Mahmud of Ghazna. From 999 to 1030, Mahmud ruled a region that is now shared by Afghanistan and Iran. Muhammad Ghuri completed the Muslim conquest of the subcontinent in the late twelfth century. He established his capital at Delhi, India, and subdued northern regions between modern Pakistan and present-day Bangladesh. His armies overthrew the Rajputs. This new empire became known as the Delhi Sultanate (kingdom).

The Delhi Sultanate slowly declined after 1398, when Mongol armies swept down from central Asia and sacked Delhi. The Delhi Sultanate survived for another century before falling in 1526 to the Mongol leader Zahir-ud-Din Muhammad.

CASTE SYSTEM

Hinduism uses the caste system to divide its social classes. The basic castes are called *varnas*, or colors. Varnas have subcastes known as *jâtis*. There are thousands of subcastes in India, each with its own administrative structure.

At the top of the system are the Brahmins (priests and teachers). Next are the Ksatriyas (warriors) and then the Vaisyas (farmers, merchants, and craftspeople). Below these are the Sudras (laborers). At the bottom of the social system are the Untouchables. The Untouchables work in professions considered too polluted to be performed by caste Hindus. These include dealing with bodies of dead animals, leatherworking, and cleaning up garbage and human waste.

Babur

Zahir-ud-Din Muhammad, called Babur by his followers, united northern India, Pakistan, and Bangladesh under his rule (1526–1530). This laid the foundations of the Mughal Empire. (Mughal is derived from the word Mongol.) The empire traded heavily, especially with Portugal, and generated immense wealth. In addition, its policy of religious tolerance calmed the Hindus, who had feared that the Islamic Mughals would try to convert them.

The Mughal Empire flourished under Babur's grandson Akbar, who reigned from 1556 to 1605. Akbar cultivated the goodwill of the Hindus, especially the Rajputs, by placing some of them in high positions in his government. Akbar also encouraged intermarriage between Rajputs and Muslims. Trade expanded to include Britain and France.

Akbar's immediate successors continued his policy of religious tolerance. But when Alamgir (also called Aurangzeb) seized the throne in 1658, the new emperor returned to strict Islamic ways. He taxed Hindus heavily and destroyed their temples.

This illustration from the Mughal Empire depicts **Emperor Akbar** atop an elephant.

British Expansion and Rule

Following the death of Alamgir in 1707, the Mughal Empire began to collapse. Regional rivalries between Hindu and Muslim princedoms (independent states ruled by princes) erupted all over the subcontinent. Britain and France each made alliances with local rulers in the interest of trade on the continent. By the mid-eighteenth century, the British East India Company was playing a strong part in the politics of the Indian subcontinent.

Local princes, in turn, took advantage of the rivalry between the British and the French to gain power over other local rulers. For example, the Sikhs—a religious community that had formed an independent realm—took over kingdoms in Kashmir and Peshawar. Under their leader, Ranjit Singh, the Sikhs developed a strong administration centered in Lahore.

Throughout the 1700s and early 1800s, the British took control of Sindh, Hyderabad, and Khairpur princedoms. By 1849 Punjab was completely under British rule. Britain also gained authority over Baluchistan by treaty in 1854. Over the next century, Britain steadily extended its influence.

The British East India Company exercised political power on the subcontinent without the direct involvement of the British government. But between 1857 and 1858, rebellions against British rule erupted in eastern and central India. British troops finally defeated the Indian rebels. As a result of these conflicts, however, responsibility for and rule of India was transferred to the British government in 1858.

Britain promised not to interfere in the religious affairs of the people, and it gathered the support of local leaders for its colonial administration. A resident official of the British government, usually the governor-general, indirectly controlled the princely states—

TRADE WITH EUROPE

Europeans had traded with Pakistan and India in ancient times. They renewed their contact in 1498, when the Portuguese navigator Vasco da Gama visited the subcontinent. The Portuguese established commercial links and brought Mughal goods to Europe throughout the sixteenth century. Reports of the wealth of the Mughal Empire stirred Britain, France, and the Netherlands to compete with Portugal for the empire's trade. In the 1600s, the British East India Company established commercial outposts on the Indian subcontinent. Mughal emperors and the trading companies profited from the exchange of spices and textiles.

During the **Sepoy Rebellion** of 1857, Indian troops in the British army rose up against the British. The rebels lost, but their actions represented the growing wish for independence among the region's native population.

territories under British military protection but ruled by local princes. The governor-general held executive and legislative authority, with district officers handling local administrative matters. In the northwestern regions of the subcontinent, British holdings included Sindh, Punjab, and parts of the North-West Frontier Province (NWFP). Baluchistan, Gilgit, and Jammu and Kashmir were princely states.

Opposition to British rule emerged slowly, beginning with the formation of the Indian National Congress in 1885. The congress originally wanted self-rule for India within the British Empire. Over several decades, the congress, whose members were mostly Hindus, became the only organization that had widespread national support.

Muslims formed the second largest group in India's population in the late 1800s, but they were greatly outnumbered by Hindus. The British supported the creation of the All-India Muslim League in 1906 as a counterbalance to the Indian National Congress. Mohammed Ali Jinnah, whom Pakistanis call Quaid-i-Azam, or Great Leader, headed the league. Under his leadership, the league grew into an influential political party. Jinnah strongly advocated Hindu-Muslim cooperation. Like Mohandas K. Gandhi—who headed the Indian National Congress—Jinnah supported a united, independent Indian state.

Mohammed Ali Jinnah led the All-India Muslim League. The league was one of the main groups to spearhead India's push for independence.

Road to Independence

More than one million soldiers from the subcontinent fought with British troops in Europe and the Middle East during World War I (1914–1918). Nationalist Indian leaders cooperated with Britain, in part because they expected that Britain would give them greater postwar involvement in the government. The Government of India Act of 1919, however, made few changes and did not satisfy India's Muslim or Hindu leaders.

The Indian National Congress continued to attract millions of Indians and sought to unite religious and ethnic groups. But Jinnah and other Muslim activists, such as Allama Muhammad Iqbal, grew disillusioned with the congress's policies. Convinced that Muslims would never receive their full rights in a Hindu-dominated India, Jinnah announced a plan in 1929 for a separate Muslim voter roll. In 1930 Iqbal outlined the concept of a federated India, in which a separate Muslim state—consisting of Punjab, the NWFP, Sindh, and Baluchistan—would exist.

After negotiating with various Indian leaders, Britain passed a new Government of India Act in 1935. This new legislation established independent provincial governments. The Indian National Congress dominated most of these regional councils.

At the outset of World War II (1939–1945), Britain declared itself and its empire, including India, to be at war with Germany. Because

Britain had not involved the Indian National Congress in this decision, the congress refused to cooperate. The Muslim League, on the other hand, supported Britain during the war in the hope of gaining postwar support for the Muslim community. They especially wanted to establish a separate Muslim nation called Pakistan, a name formed from the first letters of regions in the northwest.

The Muslim League passed a declaration of independence, called the Lahore Resolution, on March 23, 1940. This resolution declared that the British and Indian governments should form independent states of the areas where Muslims comprised a majority. The league argued that Partition (the division of India into Hindu and Muslim territories) was the only way to ensure Muslim social, political, and economic equality.

After World War II ended, the British tried to find common ground between the Indian National Congress and the Muslim League. But the two groups could not agree on a post-independence government. The British began to view Partition as the only solution.

Partition and Independence

In June 1947, Britain announced a plan to establish two nations from its holdings on the subcontinent. India would have a Hindu majority, and Pakistan, a Muslim majority. The main religious group in a given region would determine to which nation the territory would belong.

Members of the **conference on Partition** met on June 7, 1947, to discuss terms for the creation of Muslim and Hindu territories.

Muslims of the northwestern regions chose to form West Pakistan, and Muslims of East Bengal made up East Pakistan. More than 1,000 miles (1,609 km) of Indian territory separated the two wings of the new nation. The British plan allowed princely states to join either India or Pakistan or to remain independent.

The Indian National Congress and the Muslim League agreed to the plan, despite its difficulties. In August 1947, Britain formally acknowledged that India and Pakistan were independent. Both became dominions within the British Commonwealth—that is, self-governing nations that acknowledged the British monarch as their symbolic head.

Bloody riots accompanied Partition, particularly in Punjab, as more than 10 million people moved across the new boundaries to the country of their choice. Estimates indicate that between 250,000 and 500,000 Muslims died as their new nation was taking shape. Muslim immigrants, called *muhajirs*, moved from their birthplaces in central India, in East Punjab, or in West Bengal to either wing of the new Muslim nation.

Aside from religion, the Bengalis of East Pakistan had little connection to Pakistanis in West Pakistan. In particular, East Pakistan felt

In August 1947, thousands of Indian Muslims boarded trains in New Delhi, India, to begin a new life in Pakistan.

economically exploited by West Pakistan, especially by the dominant Punjabi population. Long the source of jute (a fiber used to make rope), Bengal became divided between jute growers and manufacturers. Jute farms lay in East Pakistan, but the factories that processed the crop were located in the Indian state of West Bengal. As a result, Bengali Muslims of East Pakistan lost access to the machinery needed to process their crop.

Despite these setbacks, the government of the Dominion of Pakistan established itself in Karachi, the nation's first capital city. Jinnah became the first governor-general of Pakistan, and Liaquat Ali Khan served as his prime minister. Jinnah's popularity allowed him to combine the offices of head of state, leader of the Muslim League, and governor-general into one office.

Another challenge for the new nation was the princely state of Jammu and Kashmir. The area had been a predominantly Muslim realm but was ruled by a Hindu prince. The government of Pakistan believed that the majority Muslim population should become part of a Muslim nation. Muslim militants from the NWFP caused disturbances in Jammu and Kashmir. The region's Hindu leader agreed to join the Indian union in return for military assistance to repel the militants. India claimed the entire region, but Pakistan refused to accept the prince's pro-Indian decision. The United Nations (UN) established a cease-fire line that snaked through Jammu and Kashmir. India received 63 percent of the area, while the remaining 37 percent went to Pakistan. (Despite continued conflict and ethnic violence, this division has remained intact.)

Jinnah died in September 1948. Political instability followed his death and brought about frequent party realignments and cabinet changes. Political leaders could not agree about what it meant to be a Muslim nation. Thus, the people continued to think of themselves as Bengalis, Punjabis, and Sindhi instead of as Pakistanis. Over the next seven years, with no leader of Jinnah's stature, Pakistan had six prime ministers. It could not achieve the internal stability necessary for economic and political progress.

Coups and Constitutions

In the late 1940s, an assembly had been formed to write a constitution acceptable to both wings of Pakistan. Sharp divisions within the country became evident as years passed without a written document that declared the nation's ideas and goals. Finally, in 1956 the assembly produced a constitution that changed Pakistan from a dominion to an Islamic republic.

But the various emerging political parties—including the Republican Party, the Awami League, and the United Front—disagreed

General Ayub Khan *(second from right)* met with U.S. president John Kennedy *(right)*, Vice President Lyndon Johnson *(second from left)*, and Secretary of State Dean Rusk *(left)* in 1961.

about the constitution's election rules and about the distribution of power. Regional violence erupted in Baluchistan, in the NWFP, and in East Pakistan. The economy declined because of this disruption, and Pakistanis lost confidence in their government.

In 1958 a group of senior military officers took over the nation's affairs. President Iskander Mirza, General Ayub Khan, and senior military officers proclaimed a coup (a swift, forceful change of government). The president declared martial law (rule by the military), dismissing both the central and provincial governments. Within three weeks of the coup, however, the military exiled Mirza to Great Britain. General Khan named himself chief martial law administrator and became a military dictator.

General Khan's administration brought many changes. Politicians and bureaucrats convicted of corruption were replaced by the general's supporters. More rights were granted to women, including the right to run for government office. The new regime built many schools and designed projects to improve health standards, industry, defense, and communications. Rawalpindi (the headquarters of the army) temporarily replaced Karachi as the capital of Pakistan until the new capital in Islamabad was completed.

In 1962 a committee drafted a new constitution. The constitution arranged for members of local councils, called Basic Democracies, to elect the president for the general population. Soon after the constitution took effect, Ayub Khan suspended martial law and scheduled new elections for 1965. After the 1965 elections, a majority of Basic Democrats chose Ayub Khan as president.

By 1968 internal opposition to Ayub Khan had grown due to his seemingly unfair treatment of the provinces. Even members of the military—Khan's traditional supporters—began to express discontent. Foreign minister Zulfikar Ali Bhutto resigned his post to organize the Pakistan People's Party (PPP).

In 1969 another coup—this time carried out by Mohammad Yahya Khan, commander in chief of the army—forced Ayub Khan's resignation. Yahya Khan suspended the constitution and became head of a new regime of martial law. Eventually, Yahya Khan named himself president. Elections were scheduled for the following year.

The Pakistan People's Party was founded in 1967 under the slogan "Islam is our faith; democracy is our polity; socialism is our economy; all power to the people." Since its creation, the party has risen to power several times under the leadership of Zulfikar Ali Bhutto and later his daughter Benazir.

Birth of Bangladesh

The 1970 elections for national and provincial assemblies brought two opposing ideas and political personalities to the public's attention. In West Pakistan, Bhutto and his PPP won a majority of votes, while Mujibur Rahman (called Mujib) and the Awami League overwhelmingly dominated East Pakistan. Bhutto advocated economic reforms and centralized authority, while Mujib wanted self-rule for East Pakistan.

Bhutto had Mujib arrested and taken to West Pakistan. Mujib's supporters fled to India, where they set up a government-in-exile to fight for the independent Bengali nation of Bangladesh. Between March and December of 1971, Pakistani troops clashed with the Bengali Liberation Army. By late 1971, estimates indicated that nearly eight million East Pakistanis had fled the conflict by crossing the border into India. Violence, famine, and disease threatened those who remained.

Zulfikar Ali Bhutto

Pakistan conducted air raids into India's territory in search of guerilla fighters. In response, Indian forces fought alongside the Bengalis, taking Dacca—the main city in East Pakistan—in December 1971. India recognized the provisional government of the new nation of Bangladesh on December 6, and

Indian troops moved in to secure East Pakistan on December 17, 1971, the day after Pakistan surrendered the territory. East Pakistan became the independent nation of Bangladesh.

Pakistan's army surrendered on December 16. Twenty-four hours later, India's prime minister, Indira Gandhi, called a cease-fire, and Yahya Khan resigned.

If you'd like to learn more about the history and government of Pakistan, go to vgsbooks.com for links where you can find out details about the ancient Indus Valley civilization, Harappa; learn more about Mughal art and architecture; and find up-to-date information on the current Pakistani government.

Bhutto and Zia

Following the loss of its eastern wing, the government in West Pakistan asked Bhutto to rule what remained of Pakistan. Bhutto established friendly contacts with the Soviet Union and several Arab states. He and Indira Gandhi signed the Simla Accord, which provided for the return of ninety thousand Pakistani prisoners of war. In exchange, Bhutto assured India that Pakistan would not attempt to take Jammu and Kashmir by force. Meanwhile, after East Pakistan gained independence, a group of nationalists in Baluchistan sought self-rule. In 1973 the Pakistan army put down a rebellion by militant Baluchis, and violence ensued.

After thirteen years under military rule, the people of Pakistan wanted Bhutto to improve economic and social conditions. Bhutto promised land reform, and he nationalized (changed from private to

government ownership) much of the industrial sector. In general, he was able to revive the nearly collapsed economy that he had inherited. He also aimed to make Pakistan a one-party state. To achieve this, he needed a landslide victory in a general election, an event that would demonstrate the PPP's countrywide popularity.

Bhutto held elections in 1977, manipulating the results to assure the PPP's victory. This action led to widespread public discontent, and riots broke out. Bhutto declared martial law in Lahore, Karachi, and Hyderabad. In July 1977, the situation spun out of control. The army seized power and jailed Bhutto. Bhutto was tried, found guilty, and executed in April 1979. Meanwhile, General Mohammed Zia ul-Haq proclaimed himself chief martial law administrator.

Zia focused his efforts on moving Pakistan closer to Islamic ideals. Islamic laws, called Sharia, were used to settle legal disputes. Wardens ensured that Muslims prayed the required number of times each day. Women lost some of the rights they had gained under Ayub Khan.

◉ Scandal and Reform

In 1985, after assuming the presidency, Zia ended martial law. He allowed political parties to function openly and called for elections to the National Assembly (the lower legislative house). Meanwhile, Benazir Bhutto, daughter of former prime minister Zulfikar Ali Bhutto, returned to Pakistan from exile in 1986 and became the leader of the PPP.

In May 1988, Zia dissolved the cabinet, dismissed the prime minister, and suspended the National Assembly. He cited widespread corruption as his reason, although others believed his action was politically motivated. The president announced that new elections would be held in November. In August 1988, President Zia and several top-ranking army officers died in an airplane crash. The disaster left Pakistan without strong leadership at the government and military levels.

Benazir Bhutto

In November 1988, Ishaq Khan was elected president. The PPP won the largest number of seats of any of the nation's political organizations. The president named Benazir Bhutto prime minister, and she became the first female head of an Islamic state. Hampered by opposing political forces, ethnic unrest, and political inexperience, Bhutto was unable to address the nation's many problems. In 1990 President Ishaq Khan, backed by the military, dissolved Benazir Bhutto's government and charged her administration with widespread corruption. Nawaz Sharif then became prime minister.

In May 1991, the National Assembly passed laws that made Pakistan's government consistent with Islamic law. But political tensions continued to plague the government. In 1993 President Khan dismissed Sharif and dissolved the National Assembly. But Pakistan's Supreme Court ruled that Khan's act was unconstitutional and ordered the old government be restored.

Pakistan's army intervened to negotiate an end to the crisis. The president and prime minister resigned, and the legislature was dissolved. An interim government took control of Pakistan until elections could be held. In October 1993, Benazir Bhutto again was elected prime minister. The following month, Farooq Leghari was elected president.

During her term, Bhutto decreased Pakistan's budget deficit and improved relations with the United States, which had concerns about Pakistan's potential to create nuclear weapons. Despite these positive changes, Bhutto was dismissed again in late 1996 on charges of corruption and incompetence. President Leghari appointed an interim prime minister and called for new elections. Nawaz Sharif was reelected to the post.

Old and New Issues

Tensions between Pakistan and India escalated in 1998, when Pakistan conducted nuclear weapons tests in response to India's weapons testing that same year. The following year, Pakistani troops seized Indian territory in Jammu and Kashmir. Prime Minister Sharif agreed to

Prime Minister Nawaz Sharif *(left)* met with U.S. president Bill Clinton *(right).* They discussed U.S. sanctions against Pakistan and nuclear arms control in the region.

remove Pakistani troops from the occupied Indian lands, creating conflict between the government and the military.

The situation worsened in October 1999 when Sharif attempted to dismiss General Pervez Musharraf from his position as army chief of staff. Musharraf and his supporters took control of the government and declared martial law. Sharif was exiled to Saudi Arabia. In response to the coup and the 1998 nuclear testing, the United States imposed trade sanctions against Pakistan.

Musharraf declared himself president in June 2001. That same year, Pakistan became an unexpected ally of the United States. On September 11, 2001, terrorists attacked the World Trade Center in New York City and the Pentagon in Washington, D.C., killing thousands of Americans and many foreign nationals.

The U.S. government and much of the world blamed a terrorist organization known as al-Qaeda, an informal international network of terrorist groups led by a former Saudi Arabian citizen, Osama bin Laden. At that time, bin Laden was using Pakistan's neighbor Afghanistan as his base for terrorist activities. Pakistan had long been an important political ally of Afghanistan.

The United States organized an international coalition to wage war on terrorism. It demanded that Afghanistan hand over bin Laden and other terrorist leaders. When negotiations between Afghanistan and the coalition broke down, the United States began an extensive military campaign. Pakistan found itself in the middle of this conflict.

Despite protests from some Pakistani militant groups and the Afghan government, President Musharraf promised full cooperation to American forces. As part of this promise, Pakistan closed its borders to Afghan refugees and agreed to allow the U.S. military the use of its airspace. In return, the United States lifted its trade sanctions against Pakistan and provided economic aid and diplomatic backing.

While the country hopes for an economic boost from renewed trade with the United States, some Pakistanis fear this new alliance will damage the nation's relations with Afghanistan. Another concern comes from having close ethnic ties with the Afghans. Tribal groups in the NWFP have family and friends living in Afghanistan. Siding with the United States means potentially pitting family members against each other. In addition, the United States remains a skeptical ally, especially after key al-Qaeda members were found hiding in Karachi after the September 11 attacks.

Tensions over U.S. treatment of Pakistani detainees (people held for questioning about terrorist activities) escalated into violence in 2002. Angry over Pakistan's alliance with the United States, a militant group called the National Movement for the Restoration of Pakistani Sovereignty kidnapped and killed American journalist Daniel Pearl in February 2002. His death threatened the already shaky truce between the new allies. Pakistan drew further criticism in May 2002 when it conducted more nuclear missile tests.

◉ Government

When General Musharraf took over Pakistan's government in 1999, he suspended the existing constitution and established a provisional constitution that supported his military regime. Musharraf declared himself chief executive and dissolved the existing parliament. He also suspended the national and provincial assemblies.

General Pervez Musharraf *(right, with U.S. secretary of defense Donald Rumsfeld)* arrived in Washington, D.C., on February 13, 2002, just days after the kidnapping and killing of American journalist Daniel Pearl. Pakistan's relationship with the United States has created tensions in Pakistan.

The National Security Council functions as Pakistan's supreme governing body. The eight-member council, appointed by Musharraf, includes military and civilian advisers, a cabinet, and governors for all four provinces. Political parties and government bureaucracy operate under the military's watchful eye.

Musharraf kept the country's judicial system. The Supreme Court is the highest tribunal in Pakistan, and each province also has its own high court. In addition, the Federal Shariat Court, consisting of eight Muslim judges, determines whether a civil law is consistent with the laws of Islam. However, Musharraf demanded that all Supreme and High Court judges take an oath of loyalty to his government. This means that justices cannot make any orders against the chief executive or any person working under his authority.

In 2000 the Supreme Court ruled that Musharraf's government was constitutional, but it also imposed a three-year deadline (starting from October 12, 1999, the date of Musharraf's coup) to complete the transition from military to civilian rule. In November 2002, Pakistan's parliament elected Mir Zafarullah Khan Jamali as the country's new prime minister. Jamali's election is the first step toward returning to a civilian government.

THE PEOPLE

The population of Pakistan is 145 million, a figure that includes more than 2 million refugees from Afghanistan. Most Pakistanis live in rural areas and work as farmers or herders. In the country, many villages have no electricity or running water, and clothes are usually washed in the rivers or streams. Farming is the chief employment in rural areas, and many farmers continue to use traditional methods. Nomadic herders travel through the country, following their herds of livestock. They usually live in tents that they pack up and carry with them.

A growing number of people live in cities, where most work in factories or shops. Pakistan's cities continue to grow rapidly as young people move from the countryside to find work. City dwellers may work at banks, businesses, or hospitals, or they may even start their own businesses. Most city families live in bungalows or in apartment buildings. Poorer people may live in small homes. Wealthy Pakistanis usually live in the cities and are often active in politics or education.

Ethnic Groups

Ethnically, Pakistan is very diverse, and each group retains its own dialect, culture, and history. Punjabis, the nation's largest ethnic community, live in Punjab—the biggest and most fertile province in the country. Even before Partition, Punjabis dominated the economy of their region. Punjabi landowners, whose estates produce much of the nation's food and exports, have become powerful members of the government. The continued influence of Punjabis over nearly every facet of national activity has created tensions between them and the other ethnic communities in Pakistan.

The Sindhi, residents of Sindh, make up the country's second largest ethnic group. Sindh is less fertile than Punjab, and its residents farm small holdings or lease land from landlords. At independence, millions of Hindus and Sikhs left Sindh for India, and a huge influx of refugee Muslims arrived in Sindh from India. These newcomers often possessed better schooling and more technical skills than native Sindhi. Tensions exist between the "new Sindhi" and the province's native inhabitants.

Punjabi schoolchildren hang out after school in Lahore.

Pathans (or Pashtuns), who share cultural and linguistic ties with Pathans in Afghanistan, overwhelmingly populate the NWFP. Pathans have a variety of professions within the mountainous terrain of their province. The most important feature of Pathan life is the Islamic religion. The Quran, or book of Islamic holy writings, influences many aspects of Pathan society, including the times for prayer and fasting.

The southwestern area of Pakistan where the Baluchi live is rich in natural resources, particularly oil, natural gas, and copper. Pakistan's Baluchi population is mostly made up of nomadic herders, farmers, or fishers. Violence in the 1970s between the Baluchi and Pakistan's army angered even those Baluchi who had been content with life in Baluchistan. As a result, modern Baluchi strongly oppose Pakistani and Punjabi attempts to control them.

Muhajirs—people who moved from India to Pakistan at Partition—generally migrated to urban areas and greatly increased the populations of Pakistan's cities. Many muhajirs have become powerful business and political leaders. Mohammed Ali Jinnah, Liaquat Ali Khan, and Mohammed Zia ul-Haq were all muhajirs.

Language

Shortly after Partition in 1947, the government of Pakistan sought to establish a national language. This proved to be difficult because Pakistanis speak many different tongues. The main language groups are Panjabi, Pashto (the Pathan tongue), Sindhi, and Baluchi. The dialects within these groups are also quite varied. A Panjabi dialect known as Lahnda, for example, is considered so significantly different from the common Panjabi dialect that it is often classified as an entirely separate language.

The government selected Urdu as Pakistan's official language because many people who spoke different languages could readily understand it. Yet fewer than 10 percent of the nation's people speak Urdu as their primary language. Urdu is actually a blend of many languages that have Hindi as their primary grammatical base. Persian, Arabic, Turkish, and English words also contribute to the language.

⦿ Health

Living conditions in Pakistan have improved since independence, but the nation still must deal with the problems caused by inadequate health care. Limited facilities, extreme poverty, and lack of public awareness are all obstacles the health care system faces. The situation for women is generally worse than it is for men. For example, female children receive medical treatment less frequently and often are given smaller amounts of food than their brothers.

The major health dangers—disease, malnutrition, and impure water—are the same as those that plagued the country in the early and mid-1900s. Diseases like malaria, typhoid, and tuberculosis still afflict the population. Even curable ailments, such as diphtheria and measles, continue to kill Pakistani children. The infant mortality rate—the number of babies who die within their first year—is 91 deaths in every 1,000 births. Life expectancy in Pakistan is 60 years, an average figure in southern Asia. About 42 percent of the population are under the age of 15, and only 4 percent are over age 65.

To learn more about the various ethnic groups of Pakistan—including the Punjabis, Sindhi, and Pashtuns—and the most current health statistics for Pakistan, go to vgsbooks.com.

⦿ Education

Although the government guarantees every child in Pakistan a free primary education, school attendance is not required, and universal schooling has not yet been achieved. Moreover, Islamic tradition, which encourages females to remain in the home, makes it harder for girls to obtain a basic education.

Primary education starts at age five and lasts for five years. Middle school and secondary education begin at age ten and are divided into two stages of three and four years. In 2000 about 20 million Pakistani

CHILDREN

Children from poor families rarely go to school. They often work in the family business or as carpet weavers to help support the family. Some might be apprenticed to a tradesperson so that they can learn a skill. Girls usually stay home to cook, clean, and care for their younger siblings. Wealthier families hire outside help to do the household chores, so children can spend much of their time on schoolwork or at play. Girls learn how to cook and run a household, and boys learn the family business. The legal age for marriage is sixteen for girls and eighteen for boys.

children attended preprimary and primary schools, and more than 6 million were enrolled in middle and secondary schools.

Adult literacy is 44 percent—58 percent for men and 29 percent for women. In the late 1990s, the government started the National Education Policy, which aimed to further spread basic education and to eliminate illiteracy. The policy has strengthened adult literacy programs and emphasizes technical and vocational learning. One approach to expanding education has been to hold literacy classes in mosques (Islamic places of prayer). Even the smallest and most isolated villages have mosques, and they are typically in better condition than most school buildings.

Pakistan, which began with few institutions of higher learning, has almost one thousand universities, colleges, and technical training schools. The University of Punjab in Lahore and the University of Karachi are among the nation's main

University students at Punjab University in Lahore meet between classes. A growing number of **female students** is attending universities in Pakistan.

postsecondary institutions. Private universities, which better ensure well-paid employment after graduation, also exist, but the high cost of tuition limits enrollment mainly to children of wealthy families.

Family Life

Family is important in Pakistan. Pakistani families are patriarchal, meaning fathers are heads of the households. Extended families often live together, with three or four generations under one roof. Young couples, if they are financially stable, sometimes prefer to live alone.

The position of Pakistani women in society is complex. Families traditionally celebrate the birth of a son more than the birth of a daughter. Girls, especially in rural areas, do not receive the same education that boys do.

Some families even practice *purdah,* the almost complete segregation of women and men through the seclusion of women. A wife never mingles with men except for her husband and male relatives. When she leaves her home, she must wear a full-length cover known as a *burka.*

However, Pakistani women are making strides toward equality. Pakistan has appointed women ambassadors and even elected a woman to be prime minister. Some women have studied to become doctors, pilots, and business leaders.

The most frequently worn style of dress for men and women is the *shalwar-qamiz*, a combination of loose trousers and a long blouse. Women sometimes add a scarf called a *dupatta.* Outside the home, some women wear a veil or a full-length covering called a burka *(right)* in accordance with Islamic rules of modesty. Men often wear turbans or caps.

CULTURAL LIFE

Pakistan's official religion, Islam, was the basis for the country's creation as an independent nation. It is a driving force in Pakistani culture. Islam influences every aspect of Pakistani culture, from its social structure to art.

The country's past also plays a part in Pakistan's rich cultural life. Remains of Mughal architecture stand among colonial and modern buildings. And British colonialism is evident in Pakistan's most popular sports—cricket and squash. In music and literature, traditional forms such as poetry and folk songs still enjoy wide popularity among modern performers. Artists and craftspeople combine traditional forms and subject matter with modern techniques. In all, Islam remains a favorite theme.

Religion

About 97 percent of Pakistan's population is Muslim. The nation was created so that the Muslims of the subcontinent would have their own homeland. As a result, Islam holds a central place in Pakistani society, although ethnic affiliations are also important. In 1991 Pakistan's National Assembly passed laws to make the government consistent with Islamic law. The country's provisional government retained Pakistan's Sharia court, which determines if civil law is consistent with Islamic law.

Muslims believe in one Supreme Being, Allah, and that his message was brought to his people by the prophet Muhammad. Soon after Muhammad founded Islam on the Arabian Peninsula in the seventh century, the religion split into two main factions: Sunnis and Shiites. Sunni Muslims accept an elected successor to the Islamic leadership, while Shiites regard only descendants of Muhammad as legitimate leaders. Most of Pakistan's Muslims belong to the Sunni sect. Shiites are concentrated in Karachi and make up substantial parts of the religious communities in Punjab and the NWFP.

Muslims of both sects are required to pray five times daily. They also observe rules of fasting, especially during the holy month of Ramadan. They must make charitable donations and are encouraged to attempt a pilgrimage to the holy city of Mecca in Saudi Arabia once in their lifetime. Conservative Pakistani Muslims sometimes clash with religious moderates over the role of Islam in an Islamic republic. Conservatives believe that the Federal Shariat Court should be the supreme law in the land and that the Quran should be followed literally. Moderates want more balance between civil and religious regulations.

Small numbers of Hindus and Christians live in Pakistan. Laws bar them from holding public office, although they are generally free to practice their faiths. Some discrimination in employment and educational opportunities exists against non-Muslims.

◉ Holidays and Festivals

The most important time of the year for Muslims is Ramadan—the holy month of fasting. Ramadan is the ninth month of the Islamic calendar. During this month, Muslims may not eat or drink anything after the sun rises and before the sun sets. Ramadan is a time for prayer and worship.

One of Pakistan's two major festivals is the Eid al-Fitr (Small Holiday). Eid al-Fitr marks the end of Ramadan. During Eid al-Fitr, children receive gifts of clothing and money. Children's hands are decorated with *mehndi*, a reddish dye made from henna. Businesses close for the holiday, and workers receive bonuses. Families eat a special meal together, and then the men and boys gather for special prayers. Food and money are distributed to the poor.

For links to websites where you can find up-to-date statistics, current events, and cultural data—including more on food, festivals, the pilgrimage to Mecca and the other four pillars of Islam—visit vgsbooks.com.

Women **decorate their hands with mehndi** in preparation for Eid al-Fitr, an important Muslim holiday.

The second important holiday is the Eid al-Azha (Big Holiday). Eid al-Azha falls about two months after Eid al-Fitr. This holiday celebrates Abraham's willingness to sacrifice his son in obedience to Allah. Men and boys gather for special prayers, and many people sacrifice a sheep, goat, or calf. They distribute the meat to family, friends, and poor people.

Other festivals include Muhurram, the first month of the Muslim calendar, when Pakistani Muslims mourn the death of Muhammad's grandson, Imam Husain. Special services are held, and most people wear black. On the tenth day, Ashura, people march through the streets.

A couple of months after Muhurram, Pakistanis celebrate Eid Milad-un-Nabi, the birthday of Muhammad. People gather to read poems praising the prophet and schoolchildren sing *kasidas*, special poems that honor Muhammad.

Regional fairs and festivals are held throughout the year. In Punjab, people celebrate the Awami Mela (the People's Festival) in March. Artists and singers give performances, and people enjoy sporting events and livestock exhibitions. In Peshawar, tribal people gather in April to perform traditional dances or to play polo. And Lahore holds a kite festival at the beginning of March to mark the start of spring.

National holidays include Pakistan Day on March 23, which commemorates the Lahore Resolution of 1940, and August 14, Pakistan's Independence Day. Muhammed Ali Jinnah's birthday is celebrated on December 25, and the anniversary of his death is commemorated on September 11.

▶ Food

Pakistani cuisine, although often spicy, is also known for its richness. Popular dishes are pilau (cooked meat and rice), *kofta* (meatballs), and *burgh kaali march* (chicken with garlic and ginger). Sweets typically include *czardas,* made with sweet rice, nuts, and spices. *Korma* is a mixture of thin spaghetti noodles, sugar, and nuts, and *halvah* is composed of ground carrots, sugar, nuts, and spices.

Chapati—a round, flat bread usually made of whole wheat—is eaten with almost every meal in Pakistan. In poor households, chapati is often the main course. It is served with other foods spread thinly over it like butter.

FRUIT CHAAT

Any fruit in season can be used for this sweet and spicy dish.

1 banana	3-4 tablespoons sugar
1 apple	pinch of salt
1 pear	1 teaspoon ground cumin
1 peach	¼ teaspoon black pepper
1 orange	a few drops of lemon juice or orange juice
1 cup grapes	

1. Cut the fruit into bite-sized pieces and put in a medium-sized bowl.
2. In a smaller bowl, mix the sugar, salt, cumin, pepper, and juice together.
3. Add to fruit and toss.

Serves 3 to 4.

▶ Literature and Music

Of all literary forms, poetry is the most popular among Pakistanis. People memorize long passages from the works of their most popular poets—Shah Abdul Latif, Khushal Khan Khattak, Allama Muhammad Iqbal, and Faiz Ahmed Faiz. A favorite form of entertainment, especially among educated people, is the *mushaira.* Groups of twenty or more people gather at mushairas to read poetry in sessions that can go on for several hours. Rural people enjoy telling folk stories, which include plays based on legendary or historical events.

Music is also popular in Pakistan. The country's ethnic groups enjoy both classical music and folk tunes. Drums and horns are popular folk instruments, and they provide accompaniment for graceful dances such as the *luddi* and the *khattak*.

Qawwalis, the songs of Sufi poets, are also popular. They were originally sung to convert nonbelievers to Islam and to strengthen the faith of believers. Traditionally, qawwalis are sung by specially trained singers who play *sarangis* (stringed instruments). Contemporary qawwali performers may play harmoniums, instruments similar to piano accordions. Modern qawwali bands sing ancient and modern songs or even compose new music. Nusrat Fateh Ali Khan is one of Pakistan's most famous *qawwals*. His performances drew international audiences made up of both Muslims and non-Muslims.

A PAKISTANI FOLKTALE

The Greedy Monkey

Once upon a time, a monkey noticed some wheat that had fallen into a small hollow in a rock. Thrusting in his paw, he filled it with the grain. But the entrance was so narrow that he was unable to draw out his paw without letting go of some of the wheat. This, however, he was unwilling to do, greedily desiring to have it all. So he remained without any, and finally went away hungry.

A Kalash woman dressed in traditional costume **plays the flute.** The Kalash are an indigenous people who live near Chitral in northern Pakistan.

The Badshahi Mosque, built in 1673, is an excellent example of traditional Islamic architecture.

⊙ Architecture

Some of the most important examples of Pakistani architecture are its mosques. Because Islam forbids the use of representational art, geometric patterns commonly decorate the doorways, floors, and walls of mosques. In addition, the many groups that once controlled the land before it became Pakistan left beautiful architectural treasures that continue to influence modern designers.

The Badshahi Mosque in Lahore represents the height of Mughal influence. Built in 1673 by Aurangzeb Alamgir, it is a huge square building with minarets (towers) at each corner. A monumental gate greets visitors, and three marble domes top the prayer chamber opposite the gate. Intricate plasterwork of geometric patterns and floral frescoes (paintings made on freshly spread plaster) adorn the inside walls.

Mughal influence can also be found in secular buildings such as Lahore Fort, built by the emperor Akbar in the late 1500s. The fort is a testimony to the immense differences between rich and poor. In the Hall of Public Audience, the emperor could look down on the common people from a specially raised balcony. Wealthier people and nobles met with the emperor on a level floor in the hall. The luxurious Palace of Mirrors on the fort's north side, built for the empress, also shows the wealth of the empire. The palace features a row of high-domed rooms, with the ceilings decorated in mosaics of hundreds of thousands of mirror fragments.

When the British took over the area, they built many public buildings and houses, creating a style known as Mughal-Gothic. In Lahore and other cities, these British residential areas were called cantonments. Cantonments typically feature tree-lined streets, shaded gardens, and small white bungalows.

Arts and Crafts

Because Islam forbids realistic portrayals of people and places, painting and sculpture are not important art forms in Pakistan. Instead of being in art galleries, Pakistani popular art adorns the trucks and buses that run through the streets. Artists use bright colors and abstract shapes to create these unique mobile canvases. Animal motifs are also popular, and religious symbolism, such as verses from the Quran, is often part of these works.

Pakistani crafters excel at weaving, metalwork, and pottery. Through these skills, everyday objects become works of art. And while modern factories produce large quantities of these products, many craftspeople still practice techniques perfected hundreds of years ago.

Men ride a decorated bus in Peshawar, Pakistan.

Weavers working on hand looms create fine carpets or textiles using cotton or wool. Some carpet makers even use camel hair. Designs may be woven into the textile or may be painted or stamped on the cloth. Certain regions have their own special designs and symbols to indicate where the item was made.

Carpets are big business in Pakistan, and the country has become one of the world's top producers of hand-knotted carpets. Whole families may work in the business, and children are considered very valuable because their small hands can more easily tie the small knots necessary to make the complex patterns. Carpets may earn prices as high as $25,000 in Pakistan and twice that amount at stores abroad.

Metalworkers make items such as trays or jewelry. Some engrave household items, such as platters, with intricate designs or calligraphy. Others use thin wire strands of gold or silver to make jewelry or decorative ornaments. Bracelets, earrings, and necklaces are also popular forms of metalwork.

Potters make plates, vases, and other items using several traditional methods. One popular method involves engraving designs on the object and then coating it with glaze. Blue and white ceramics are also popular. Potters may also produce tiles, which are used in public buildings and mosques. Tile making is usually a family business, and techniques have been handed down for generations.

A carpet weaver at work in Lahore. Carpets are big business in Pakistan. Despite industrialization, most weavers still create carpets on hand looms.

Cricket players have some fun in Pakistan's Salt Range (located between the Indus and the Jhelum Rivers). This popular sport was introduced to Pakistan by the British.

Sports and Recreation

Pakistani athletes enjoy a variety of sports, especially cricket, field hockey, and squash. Cricket is similar to baseball. At the professional level, the Pakistani national cricket team travels and competes against international rivals such as Great Britain, India, and Australia.

Field hockey, which is like ice hockey but is played on a grass field, remains a favorite sport in Pakistan. In fact, Pakistan's field hockey teams have been considered among the best in the world. The country won gold medals at the 1960 and 1968 Olympic Games, and it has also dominated the Asian Games. Because of its widespread popularity, some schools have formed field hockey teams for girls.

Squash is played with rackets on a small indoor court. Some of Pakistan's professional players have won world championships, and player Hashim Khan wrote a standard guide book that has become internationally famous.

Other sports popular among both amateurs and professionals include polo and *kabaddi,* a type of team wrestling. Schoolchildren fly kites, play table tennis, swim, and play games. In March, schools hold a special sports day for kids, when teams compete for ribbons and trophies.

Outside of school, boys and girls rarely play together. As they get older, girls are discouraged from playing outside the house. They typically learn other skills such as embroidery, painting, and crafts.

THE ECONOMY

At the time of Partition in 1947, Pakistan's economy was almost exclusively agricultural. There were no large industries, no locally owned banks, few commercial enterprises, and only a handful of trained technicians, professional people, and skilled workers. Since Partition, new banks, businesses, and industries have sprung up, and part of the workforce has undergone technical training.

The number of jobs requiring skilled workers has risen in Pakistan, and many unskilled Pakistanis have left to take better paying jobs in other Islamic countries. More than three million Pakistanis work abroad, mostly in oil-producing countries throughout the Middle East. The economy of Pakistan benefits substantially from the foreign earnings that these laborers send home to their families.

Since 1955 Pakistan's economic development has followed a series of five-year plans. These long-range strategies name specific economic goals, identify resources, and assign priorities. To

web enhanced @ www.vgsbooks.com

achieve these aims and to create a capitalist economy, Pakistan has sometimes relied heavily on economic assistance from more developed countries, including the United States, Great Britain, Australia, New Zealand, and Canada.

The 2001 lifting of U.S. trade sanctions imposed in 1999 gave Pakistan's economy a much needed boost. The country's economy grew by more than 4 percent in 2002 and was estimated to grow about 5 percent in 2003. However, water shortages and global economic problems continue to slow the country's growth.

Pakistan's economic needs and its religious laws sometimes clash. For example, Islam forbids collecting interest on loans. But this prohibition interferes with the capitalist system that the country is trying to establish. Until Pakistan's economy grows stronger, balancing its economic needs with the laws of Islam will continue to be a challenge to Pakistan's religious and political leaders.

Agriculture

Despite advances in some industrial and technical fields, Pakistan is still a predominantly agricultural country. Agriculture provides 26 percent of the nation's yearly income and employs about 44 percent of the nation's workforce. The government has worked to modernize planting and harvesting techniques, but many farmers own small areas of land and continue to work with simple tools or by hand. The new millennium did not bring the higher yields the government had hoped for. In 2001 Pakistan's agricultural sector suffered from low rainfall and drought.

Pakistan has two principal crop seasons—Kharif and Rabi. During Kharif, sowing begins in April or May and harvesting takes place from October through December. Kharif crops include sugarcane and cotton. The Rabi season starts with planting in October and November, with harvests taking place in April and May. Wheat and oilseeds are Rabi crops.

Pakistan's principal food crops are wheat and rice. Farmers also grow other grains, such as millet, sorghum, corn, and barley. In addition to grains, chickpeas (called *gram* in Pakistan) have become an important crop. Wheat is Pakistan's most important crop and the staple food for Pakistan's people. The country's production of wheat rose from about 15 million tons (14 million metric tons) in 1990 to 21 million tons (19 million metric tons) in 1999. Severe drought and irrigation problems, however, hurt yields, and production dropped by more than 8 percent in 2000 and 2001.

Rice is another important food crop and export commodity for Pakistan. Farmers grow rice on terraces and in irrigated fields, and yields have increased with the use of better quality rice. Pakistan exports about 2 million tons (1.8 million metric tons) of rice each year, making the nation a major supplier of this grain on the world market.

Cash crops, grown on large estates for export, include cotton, sugarcane, rice, tobacco, and oilseeds. Cotton is Pakistan's most important cash crop, with exports of raw cotton reaching $116 million in 2001. That same year, exports of cotton fabrics and cotton yarn also brought in more than $600 million each.

Sugarcane, which serves as the raw material for the production of white sugar, is another major cash crop for Pakistan. After independence, the amount of land planted in sugarcane increased steadily until Pakistan began to produce too much sugar for the international market. Farmers responded by decreasing their sugarcane fields, although

A shepherd herds his sheep in the mountains of northern Pakistan.

42.6 million tons (39 million metric tons) of sugarcane were still produced in 2001.

Oilseeds and tobacco make up the remainder of Pakistan's important cash crops. The amount of farmland devoted to these crops remains relatively small, however.

Livestock raising has long been the livelihood of Pakistanis in Baluchistan and the NWFP, where the dry climate and the rugged terrain make crop cultivation impossible. Herders tend flocks of sheep and goats and may raise cattle as work animals. Grazing land is limited, and farmers have not introduced improved animal breeds into their herds. As a result, livestock raising is still a small-scale enterprise in Pakistan.

Another agricultural product important to Pakistani farmers has been opium poppies—the plants from which the narcotic drugs opium and heroin are made. The government has tried to stop the harvest of opium poppies since about 1989. Substitute crops and other incentives have helped convince opium farmers to stop growing the illegal plant, but in the 1990s some farmers in the NWFP still relied on the income

Opium poppies

generated by the crop. In 2001 Pakistan was declared "virtually poppy-free," but some small opium farms may continue to operate. In addition, drugs still travel illegally through Pakistan from neighboring Afghanistan. Laboratories that refine poppies into heroin are generally located in the NWFP near the Afghan border. Although some heroin stays in Pakistan, much of the drug crosses the border to India or is smuggled to countries in Europe, North America, and the Persian Gulf region.

Forestry and Fishing

Pakistan's forests make up only about 4.8 percent of its total land area. Though forest resources are small, forestry employs about half a million people and supplies about one-third of the nation's energy.

In 1992 the government created a twenty-five-year plan to conserve the country's natural resources. As part of this program, local and regional organizations hold tree-planting campaigns twice a year.

Logging in Pakistan has led to erosion in some areas of the country.

Fresh fish from the Arabian Sea await sale. Fishing is an important industry for coastal areas of the country.

Fishing also plays a role in Pakistan's economy. Fishing remains a major economic activity along the coast, while inland fisheries along rivers and lakes also contribute to the national income. By 2001 Pakistan's fishing sector produced 733,000 tons (665,000 metric tons). Almost 95,000 tons (86,000 metric tons) were exported to the United States (after trade sanctions were lifted), Germany, Japan, and other countries. The government is making improvements in fishing by showing people how to raise and harvest fish in hatcheries and by updating fishing equipment.

Mining and Manufacturing

Although rich in minerals, Pakistan has not taken advantage of its natural resources. The nation lacks machinery, roads, and funds to develop this sector of its economy. Large deposits of chromite, copper, bauxite, graphite, and natural gas are located in Baluchistan. The Baluchi, however, are reluctant to allow the government to extract the

Two workers oversee a mechanized loom. Pakistan's textile industry employs many people in urban areas.

minerals in Baluchistan. They fear that the revenue from the deposits would enrich only wealthy Punjabis.

Despite these difficulties, the government has allowed private and public companies to extract copper, iron ore, sulfur, gold, silver, and molybdenum (used to strengthen steel) from Baluchistan. Foreign firms provide machinery and expertise in exchange for mining rights. The government also built the Sui Gas Line, which transports natural gas from deposits in Baluchistan to major urban centers.

After independence, Pakistan vowed to industrialize rapidly. Compared to other developing countries, manufacturing in Pakistan is growing quickly. The government has worked to privatize industry and to encourage small businesses. Large companies still dominate the public sector, however. The new millennium brought huge expansions to the manufacturing sector, which grew by 7.8 percent from 2000 to 2001.

Textiles head the list of manufactured products and include both factory-made and handwoven fabrics. Other items include processed foods, petroleum products, and cement.

Using its natural gas and limestone, Pakistan produces ammonia-based fertilizers. Pakistan also manufactures large quantities of penicillin and other medical compounds from its crop of artemisia (a medicinal herb).

In both the private and public sectors of the economy, the government's principal goal is to reduce the country's dependence on foreign imports. To achieve this, Pakistan built a major steel plant in Karachi in the 1980s with the help of the Soviet Union. Other industrial complexes produce machine tools, electrical equipment, and heavy castings. Such projects are boosting the industry. In 2000 and 2001, large-scale manufacturing increased almost 8 percent.

Energy and Transportation

In the late 1940s, forests were Pakistan's main fuel base. By the 1990s, modern sources—hydroelectric power and natural gas, for example—were providing the nation with household energy. Residents in rural areas continue to use wood and dung as fuel, and much of Pakistan's landscape has been stripped of trees. Pakistan also had two nuclear reactors in use by 2001.

Commercial energy, which powers industry and transportation, comes mainly from natural gas, oil, hydroelectricity, and coal. The Tarbela Dam on the Indus River and the Mangla Dam on the Jhelum River have increased Pakistan's hydropower output. Hydroelectric power potential has not yet been fully realized, especially in the NWFP.

The lack of a well-organized transportation network hampers Pakistan's economic development. Pakistan's government has worked hard to build and improve roads. By 2001 the country had about 155,000 miles (250,00 km) of roads, up from about 106,000 miles (171,000 km) in 1990. Many of these are still unpaved, however. Few people own cars, and most rural travel is accomplished on camels, on donkeys, or on foot.

In 2000 railroads were declared the main transportation system for the country,

TARBELA DAM

The Tarbela Dam is the world's largest earth-filled dam, measuring 1.7 miles (2.7 km) in length across the top and 470 feet (143 m) tall. The dam was started on the Indus River in 1968 and was completed in 1976 at a final cost of $828 million. The dam was created to help irrigate fields and generate electricity. At full production, the Tarbela Dam should generate about one-third of the country's electricity.

GETTING AROUND

Because Pakistan's roads are underdeveloped and over-crowded, most Pakistanis do not own cars. People in the city travel by bus, train, taxi, or animal cart. Another popular method of short-distance transportation is the auto ricksha—a three-wheeled scooter that carries a driver and several passengers. Auto rickshas were introduced to Pakistan in the late 1960s. By 2000 about 95,000 of the small, colorful vehicles could be seen weaving up and down the nation's streets.

and the government made the sector its priority for expansion. By 2006 equipment and tracks should be updated to boost the economic growth and encourage national integration. About 5,500 miles (8,851 km) of railroad track crisscross Pakistan, connecting major cities.

Pakistan International Airlines handles the nation's overseas flights. International airports are located in Lahore, Peshawar, Quetta, Rawalpindi, and Karachi. Karachi also serves as the nation's main seaport. Smaller ports also exist, such as Port Qasim, which opened in the 1980s. Two new seaports are under development at Gawadar and Keti Bunder.

⊙ The Future

Pakistan's future seems uncertain. Political unrest continues to plague the nation. After General Musharraf seized power and declared martial law, he announced general elections would take place in 2001. But Musharraf has sidestepped Pakistan's constitution to stay in power. While the government elected Jamali as civilian prime minister, only time will determine whether Pakistan will make the transition from military to civilian rule.

Ethnic violence also keeps Pakistan's future on shaky ground. An upsurge of religious violence between Sunni and Shiite Muslims around Karachi has left thousands dead. Terrorist incidents in Jammu and Kashmir further strain Indo-Pakistani dealings.

To make matters worse, drought hit Pakistan in 2000 and 2001, reducing yields and tightening the economy. A new influx of Afghan refugees fleeing war with the United States and an oppressive government managed to enter the country before the government closed its borders, placing a further burden on the unstable economy.

International relations between Pakistan and its neighbors are volatile, as well. Pakistan and India have both conducted underground atomic test explosions, drawing criticism and economic sanctions from the United States and other countries. Relations with Bangladesh have also deteriorated, and President Musharraf ordered the withdrawal of its Pakistani ambassador.

On September 27, 2001, **Pakistani protesters** rallied against the U.S. attack on Afghanistan after the September 11 terrorist attacks. Many Pakistani Muslims don't approve of their government's new relationship with the United States.

While addressing the nation's economic problems, Pakistan must find a way to balance the demands of the country's various ethnic communities and religious groups. Avoiding war with India over the disputed territory of Jammu and Kashmir grows more difficult as the Jammu and Kashmir Liberation Front, backed by Muslim Kashmiris, becomes more aggressive. And its new allegiance with the United States has also brought domestic and international pressure on an already unstable situation. Until Pakistan resolves these issues, the nation's future will remain uncertain.

 Visit vgsbooks.com for up-to-date information about Pakistan's economic situation and a converter with the current exchange rate where you can learn how many Pak rupees are in a U.S. dollar.

Timeline

CA. 2500 B.C.	The Indus Civilization settles in the area that later became Pakistan.
CA. 1700 B.C.	The Indus Civilization ends suddenly.
1500s B.C.	The Aryans enter the area.
522 B.C.	Persia captures the areas of Punjab and Sindh.
400s B.C.	Taxila becomes home to the most famous university on the Indian subcontinent.
326 B.C.	Alexander the Great enters Punjab.
322 B.C.	Chandragupta Maurya establishes the Mauryan Empire.
273–232 B.C.	Emperor Asoka makes Buddhism the official religion of the Mauryan Empire.
CA. A.D. 100	Gandhara becomes a Buddhist holy land and center of Buddhist art.
711	Muslim sailors bring Islam to the Indian subcontinent.
1498	Portuguese sailor Vasco da Gama visits the Indian subcontinent. Trade with western Europe flourishes.
1526	Babur lays the foundation for the Mughal Empire.
LATE 1500s	Emperor Akbar commissions the building of Fort Lahore.
1556–1605	Emperor Akbar encourages goodwill between Hindus and Muslims.
1631	Shah Jahan commissions the Palace of Mirrors in Lahore.
1645	The Hall of Private Audience is added to Lahore Fort.
1658	Emperor Shah Jahan is forced to give up the throne. Alamgir takes control of the empire.
1673	Emperor Alamgir builds Badshahi Mosque in Lahore.
1707	Alamgir dies and the Mughal Empire collapses.
1858	The British government seizes control of the Indian subcontinent.
1885	The Indian National Congress is formed to oppose British rule.
1906	The All-India Muslim League is created.
1911	Allama Muhammad Iqbal writes his famous poem *Shikwah*.
1940	The Muslim League passes the Lahore Resolution.
1947	Pakistan achieves independence.

1954 Pakistan adopts its national anthem, "Pak Sarzameen."

1958 The military takes over Pakistan's government in a bloodless revolution.

1960 Pakistan wins a gold medal in field hockey at the Olympic Games.

1961 Construction begins on Islamabad, the new capital.

1962 A new constitution is drafted.

1968 The Tarbela Dam is built. Pakistan's field hockey team wins its second Olympic gold medal.

1969 The military stages another coup and suspends the 1962 constitution.

1971 East Pakistan becomes the independent country of Bangladesh.

1988 Benazir Bhutto becomes the first woman elected as prime minister of an Islamic nation.

1991 Pakistan's National Assembly passes laws to make the government consistent with Islamic law.

1992 Pakistan's government creates a plan to conserve the country's natural resources.

1998 Pakistan conducts nuclear weapons testing.

1999 General Pervez Musharraf seizes control of the government and suspends the constitution.

2001 After the September 11 terrorists attacks, the United States lifts its embargo against Pakistan in return for the use of Pakistan's airspace in the war on terrorism in Afghanistan. Pakistan closes its borders to Afghan refugees.

2002 A militant group, angry over the alliance with the United States, kidnaps and kills Daniel Pearl, an American journalist. Pakistan's parliament elects a civilian prime minister, Mir Zafarullah Khan Jamali.

COUNTRY NAME Islamic Republic of Pakistan

AREA 307,375 square miles (796,098 sq. km)

MAIN LANDFORMS Baluchistan Plateau, Himalaya Mountains, Hindu Kush Mountains, Indus River Valley, Karakoram Mountains, Kirthar Range, Siahan Range, Sulaiman Range, Thar Desert, Toba Kakar Range

HIGHEST POINT Tirich Mir, 25,230 feet (7,690 m) above sea level

LOWEST POINT Sea level

MAJOR RIVERS Beas, Chenab, Gilgit, Indus, Jhelum, Kabul, Ravi, Sutlej

ANIMALS Black buks, camels, chinkaras, crocodiles, deer, Himalayan black bears, hyenas, ibex, jackals, Marco Polo sheep, markhors, neelgais, snow leopards, water buffalos

CAPITAL CITY Islamabad

OTHER MAJOR CITIES Faisalabad, Hyderabad, Karachi, Lahore, Multan, Peshawar, Quetta, Rawalpindi, Sialkot

OFFICIAL LANGUAGE Urdu

MONETARY UNIT Pak Rupee. 1 Pak rupee = 100 paisa

PAKISTANI CURRENCY

Pakistan's currency is called the Pak rupee and is as steeped in history as the country. The name rupee comes from the Sanskrit *rupya*, which means "silver." Rupees were the monetary unit of Muslim India from the sixteenth century. Starting in 1671, the British East India Company minted coins copied from the local types, using the rupee as its basic unit. It wasn't until 1835, however, that the rupee was made uniform from region to region. After India achieved independence from Britain, it kept the rupee. Pakistan began minting the Pak rupee in 1948.

Fast Facts

Currency

Mohammed Ali Jinnah, the founder of Pakistan, designed Pakistan's national flag. The flag is dark green with a white bar, representing the Muslim majority and minorities, respectively. A white crescent in the center symbolizes progress, and the five-pointed star in the center represents light and knowledge. Pakistan adopted its national flag after winning independence in 1947.

Pakistan's national anthem, "Pak Sarzameen," was adopted in 1954. The three stanza song describes Pakistan as the center of faith and freedom. The poet Abul Asar Hafeez Jullundhri composed the lyrics for the anthem, and the composer Ahmed Chagla wrote the tune. The anthem is written in Urdu, Pakistan's official language. Below is an English translation of the lyrics.

"Pak Sarzameen"
Blessed be the sacred land,
Happy be the bounteous realm,
Symbol of high resolve,
Land of Pakistan.
Blessed be thou citadel of faith.
The Order of this Sacred Land
Is the might of the brotherhood of the people.
May the nation, the country, and the State
Shine in glory everlasting.
Blessed be the goal of our ambition.
This flag of the Crescent and the Star
Leads the way to progress and perfection,
Interpreter of our past, glory of our present,
Inspiration of our future,
Symbol of Almighty's protection.

 For a link where you can listen to Pakistan's national anthem, "Pak Sarzameen," go to vgsbooks.com.

BENAZIR BHUTTO (b. 1953) In 1988 Benazir Bhutto became the first woman to head the government of a Muslim country when she was sworn in as Pakistan's prime minister. She served as prime minister from 1988 to 1990 and from 1993 to 1996. Bhutto struggled to make improvements in health, social welfare, and education, as well as to expand the role of women in Pakistani society. Born in Karachi, she went on to study at Radcliffe College and Oxford University before becoming head of the Pakistan People's Party. She has written several books, including *Daughter of Destiny*.

SUBRAHMANYAN CHANDRASEKHAR (1910–1995) Subrahmanyan Chandrasekhar was a scientist born in Lahore. He studied in India and England before moving to Chicago, Illinois. His work focused on the structure of stars and black holes. He received the Nobel Prize for physics in 1983 for his work, which he described in "The Mathematical Theory of Black Holes."

ALLAMA MUHAMMAD IQBAL (1877–1938) Born in Sialkot, Allama Muhammad Iqbal was an Islamic poet and scholar known as Shaere-Mashriq (Poet of the East). Iqbal believed that a separate state should be established for the Muslims of the Indian subcontinent. His writings promoted the Quran as not only a religious book but also as a foundation for a social and political infrastructure. His works include *Shikwah* (*The Complaint*); *Jawab-e shikwah* (*Answer to the Complaint*); and *Khizr-e rah* (*The Guide*).

SHAH JAHAN (1592–1666) Shah Jahan was born in Lahore. He ruled the Mughal Empire from 1628 to 1658. During his reign, art and architecture flourished. Some of the most famous and impressive Mughal structures were built on his orders, including the famous Taj Mahal in India and Lahore Fort in Pakistan. Mughal portraiture and illustration also reached their peak at his court.

MOHAMMED ALI JINNAH (1876–1948) Mohammed Ali Jinnah, known as the founder of Pakistan, was born in Karachi. As a young man, he became a lawyer and eventually entered politics in 1905. During his political career, Jinnah was known as a successful lawyer, an ambassador of Hindu-Muslim unity, and a freedom fighter. His demand for an independent Muslim nation eventually led to the founding of Pakistan. In 1947 he was nominated to be the first governor-general of Pakistan.

HASHIM KHAN (b. 1916) Hashim Khan is one of the most famous squash players in the world. Born in the village of Nawakille near the Khyber Pass, Khan began playing squash professionally at age twelve. At the age of thirty-five, Khan became an international phenomenon when he won the 1951 British Open and defended his title for six straight years. He later wrote a book, *Squash Racquets, The Khan Game,* that has become a standard guide for squash players around the world.

IMRAN KHAN (b. 1952) Imran Khan is considered one of the best cricket players in the world. Born in Lahore, Kahn became a star player during the 1980s. By the time he retired in 1987, he had won many awards. In 1989 he was declared international cricketer of the year and eventually became known as the best all rounder in the world. He came out of retirement in 1988 and led Pakistan to victory in the World Cup in 1992.

NUSRAT FATEH ALI KHAN (1948–1997) Nusrat Fateh Ali Kahn was considered the most important qawwal musician of his time and the most famous Pakistani singer. Born in Lyallpur in Punjab, he made his first recording in 1973. Between 1973 and 1993, Khan released more than fifty albums on Pakistani, British, American, and Japanese labels. Khan created an international following in the 1990s by collaborating with musicians such as Eddie Vedder of Pearl Jam and Peter Gabriel.

NAFIS SADIK (b. 1929) Born in Jaunpur, India, Dr. Nafis Sadik was appointed as undersecretary-general of the United Nations Population Fund (UNFPA) in 1987, making her the first woman to head a major UN program. She served in that position until her retirement in 2000. During her career, Dr. Sadik focused on directly involving women in making and enforcing political policy. Since January 2001, Dr. Sadik has served as special adviser to the UN secretary-general.

SHAHZIA SIKANDER (b. 1969) Shahzia Sikander is an artist born in Lahore. She studied at Lahore's National College of Arts and at the Rhode Island School of Design in Providence, Rhode Island. Trained in miniature, Sikander has had exhibits around the world, including the United States, Europe, and Pakistan. Her works incorporate both Hindu and Muslim elements.

OZZIR ZUBY (1921–2001) Ozzir Zuby was an artist and writer born in Kasur. Zuby's paintings and sculptures featured legendary heroes and heroines of Pakistan, and he developed a sculptural calligraphy. A style of calligraphy, Khat-i-Zuby, is named after him. In addition to his many literary contributions, he also founded a school of decor, the first of its kind in Pakistan.

BADSHAHI MOSQUE Built by Emperor Aurangzeb (Alamgir) in 1674, Lahore's Badshahi Mosque is considered the height of Mughal architecture. The intricate floral frescoes decorating the ceilings are important examples of Islamic painting.

KIRTHAR NATIONAL PARK Visitors to this park in Sindh can climb Karchat Hill, explore the carved tombs at Taung, or see the prehistoric remains Koh-Tarash. Flora and fauna also abound.

LAHORE FORT Highlights of this Mughal structure include the Pearl Mosque, the Hall of Public Audience, and the Palace of Mirrors.

MAKLI HILL Sindh's Makli Hill is the largest necropolis (city of the dead) in the world, with more than one million graves, tombs, and mausoleums.

MOHENJO-DARO This archaeological site features the ruins of a four-thousand-year-old city from the Indus civilization. A museum at the site offers information about life in prehistoric Pakistan.

NATIONAL MUSEUM One of the few museums in Pakistan, the National Museum in Karachi houses artifacts from the Indus civilization, a 1,500-year-old Buddhist sculpture, Hindu and Muslim artwork, coins, and manuscripts.

OLD CITY, RAWALPINDI Visitors can wander through Rawalpindi's maze of streets to see Hindu and Sikh temples, Muslim shrines, and historical houses.

RAWALPINDI CANTONMENT This former British residential area features sites from the country's colonial days, including a Gothic church, the Army Museum, and Ayub National Park.

SHALIMAR GARDENS Built by Shah Jahan in 1642, this Lahore sight is the only remaining example of a Mughal garden on the Indian subcontinent. It features three terraces of shaded walks, ponds, fountains, and pavilions, as well as flowers and fruit trees.

TAXILA MUSEUM The museum features an extensive collection of Gandharan Buddhist art, a coin collection, and artifacts from ancient Taxila.

Buddhism: a religion founded by Siddhartha Gautama (Buddha) in India in 500 B.C. Buddhism teaches that the way to enlightenment is through meditation and self-knowledge

cantonment: a self-contained residential area created by the British during the colonial era

delta: a triangular, fertile area of land where one or more rivers spread out into several outlets

ghazal: a Pakistani poem set to slow, melodious music

Hinduism: a religion founded by Aryans who migrated to India in 500 B.C. Hinduism's sacred texts are called the Vedas, and Hindus believe that all living things are part of the divine.

Islam: a religion based on the prophet Muhammad's teaching and founded in the seventh century A.D. Islam's holy book is the Quran, which holds the five fundamental religious duties (or pillars) for its followers.

mehndi: a reddish paste made from henna, the powdered leaves of an Asian shrub. The paste is used to decorate children's hands during certain holidays.

monsoon: a seasonal wind that typically blows from the southwest and is often accompanied by heavy rains

mosque: an Islamic place of prayer

muhajir: a Muslim immigrant who moved from India to Pakistan at Partition

Muslim: a follower of Islam

qawwali: a mystical song that aims to strengthen the faith of believers or to convert nonbelievers. Qawwalis praise Allah, the prophet Muhammad, or Muslim saints.

refugee: a person forced to flee his or her country due to political upheaval

Sufism: Islam's mystic tradition. Sufis are holy people who believe that fasting and self-denial are the true path to Allah.

Selected Bibliography

Blood, Peter R., ed. *Pakistan: A Country Study.* Washington, D.C.: Federal Research Division, Library of Congress, 1995.
This book examines the political, economic, and social systems of Pakistan.

Bloom, Jonathan M., and Sheila Blair. *Islamic Arts.* London: Phaidon Press Limited, 1997.
Bloom covers the history of Islamic art as well as the various media in which Islamic artists work.

Caesar, Farah E. *Islam: Beliefs and Observances.* Hauppage, NY: Barron's Educational Series, 2000.
Learn more about the history and beliefs of Islam, as well as its role as a cultural and political force.

CountryWatch. February 26, 2002.
<http://www.countrywatch.com/cw_country.asp?vcountry=131> (February 26, 2002).
CountryWatch includes information about Pakistan such as political history, economic conditions, environmental issues, and social customs.

Europa World Year Book. Vol. 2. London: Europa Publications Ltd., 2001.
The article covering Pakistan includes recent events, vital statistics, and economic information.

Hannigan, Des. "Pakistan." *In India, Pakistan, and the Himalayas.* Hampshire, England: AA Publishing, 2001.
The author provides a firsthand account of traveling along Pakistan's Karakoram Highway, an 800-mile-long (1,287-km) stretch that passes by some of the world's highest mountain peaks.

Islamic Republic of Pakistan. 2002.
<http://www.pak.gov.pk/> (February 26,2002).
The official site for the government of Pakistan, this website features current press releases, major news events, and vital statistics for the country.

Keay, John. *India: A History.* New York: Atlantic Monthly Press, 2000.
This book covers the history of the Indian subcontinent, from the ancient Indus Valley civilization to modern events in both India and Pakistan.

Population Reference Bureau. February 1, 2002.
<http://www.prb.org> (February 24, 2002).
The bureau offers current population figures, vital statistics, land area, and more. Special articles cover the latest environmental and health issues that concern each country.

Shaw, Isobel. *Pakistan Handbook.* Chico, CA: Moon Publications, 1998.
Shaw offers highlights and hints for travelers.

Sheehan, Sean. *Pakistan.* New York: Marshall Cavendish, 1994.
This book for younger readers includes chapters on the language, arts, and recreational activities of Pakistan's people.

Talbot, Ian. *Pakistan: A Modern History.* **New York: St. Martin's Press, 1998.**
Talbot examines Pakistan since Partition, including conflicting regional and cultural interests, the refugee situation, and Indo-Pakistani relations.

Turner, Barry, ed. *The Statesman's Yearbook: The Politics, Cultures, and Economics of the World, 2002.* **New York: Macmillan Press, 2001.**
This resource features information about Pakistan's historical events, industry and trade, climate and topography, as well as suggestions for further reading.

The World Factbook. **January 1, 2001.**
<**http://www.cia.gov/cia/publications/factbook/geos/pk.html**> **(February 24, 2002).**
This website features up-to-date information about the people, land, economy, and government of Pakistan. Transnational issues are also briefly covered.

World Gazetteer. **February 15, 2002.**
<**http://www.gazetteer.de**> **(February 24, 2002).**
The World Gazetteer offers population information about cities, towns, and places of Pakistan, including its administrative divisions.

Yusufali, Jabeen. *Pakistan: An Islamic Treasure.* **Minneapolis: Dillon Press, 1990.**
Special chapters include legends and beliefs, festivals and events, and Pakistanis in the United States.

Ali, Ahmed, ed. *The Golden Tradition; An Anthology of Urdu Poetry.* New York: Columbia University Press, 1973.
A collection of Pakistani poems.

Gordon, Matthew S. *Islam.* New York: Facts on File, 2001.
Learn more about Islam's basic tenets as well as its history and its role in politics.

Hi Pakistan
Website: <http://www.hipakistan.com/>
This website features Pakistani headline news, sports, music, and a kid's corner.

Kipling, Rudyard. *Kim.* 1901. Reprint. New York: Alfred A. Knopf, 1995.
Kipling's famous novel tells the tale of an orphan boy living on the streets of Lahore in the nineteenth century. Kim eventually sets out on a quest that brings him into the Indian Secret Service.

Kuklin, Susan. *Iqbal Masih and the Crusaders against Child Slavery.* New York: Henry Holt, 1998.
This book describes the life of Iqbal Masih, a young Pakistani boy sold into slavery at age four. After gaining his freedom six years later, he became an activist and speaker.

Lessing, Doris. *The Wind Blows Away Our Words.* New York: Vintage Books, 1987.
Lessing's work shows the life of Afghan refugees living in Pakistan.

Mittmann, Karin, and Zafar Ihsan. *Culture Shock! Pakistan.* London: Kuperard, 1991.
Learn tips about Pakistani customs.

Mumtaz, Khawar. *Women of Pakistan: Two Steps Forward, One Step Back?* London: Zed Books, 1987.
Read more about the roles and rights of women in Pakistan.

Rushdie, Salman. *Midnight's Children.* New York: A. A. Knopf, 1995.
Rushdie's prize-winning novel tells the story of two children, one Muslim and one Hindu. They are born at the stroke of midnight on August 15, 1947, the moment at which India became an independent nation. The children are switched in the hospital, eventually disrupting both families.

Sidhwa, Bapsi. *The Crow Eaters.* New York: St. Martin's Press, 1981.
This novel looks at Pakistan's Parsi community, including its customs and beliefs. When a Parsi family moves from their village to the city of Lahore, they quickly learn how complicated city life can be.

Staples, Suzanne Fisher. *Shabanu: Daughter of the Wind.* New York: A. A. Knopf, 1989.
Eleven-year-old Shabanu must choose between a marriage she does not want or disgracing her family.

Further Reading and Websites

TIMEasia.com
Website: <http://www.time.com/time/asia/>

This online version of *Time* magazine focuses on current events happening in Asia and the Pacific.

vgsbooks.com
Website: <http://www.vgsbooks.com>

Visit vgsbooks.com, the homepage of the Visual Geography Series®. You can get linked to all sorts of useful on-line information, including geographical, historical, demographic, cultural, and economic websites. The vgsbooks.com site is a great resource for late-breaking news and statistics.

Index

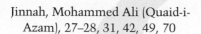

Captions for photos appearing on cover and chapter openers:

Cover: Buses await inspection at a checkpoint in the Khyber Pass.

pp. 4–5 Merchants at an outdoor market in Karachi converse in front of a friend's stall.

pp. 8–9 Snowcapped peaks dominate the skyline in northern Pakistan's mountainous region.

pp. 40–41 Pakistani children pose for a camera.

pp. 46–47 During one of five daily prayer times, Muslims kneel facing in the direction of the holy city of Mecca in Saudi Arabia.

pp. 56–57 Wheat fields are surrounded by jagged mountians.

Photo Acknowledgments
The images in this book are used with the permission of: Izzet Keribar/Atlas Geographic, pp. 4–5, 52; PresentationMaps.com, pp. 6, 12; © TRIP/F. Good, pp. 8–9, 56–57; © John Elk III, pp. 10, 19; © TRIP/J. Highet, pp. 11, 14, 16–17, 59 (top); © TRIP/Trip, pp. 13, 44, 54, 59 (bottom); © Ralph A. Clevenger/ CORBIS, p. 15; © Atlas/Atlas Geographic, pp. 18, 42; © The Art Archive/ Archaeological Museum Naples / Dagli Orti, 22; © The Art Archive/Musèe des Arts Dècoratifs Paris / Dagli Orti, p. 23; © Hulton|Archive, 25 (top), 28, 29, 30 32, 33, 34–35, 37; © Victoria & Albert Museum, London/Art Resource, NY, p. 25 (bottom); © Bettmann/CORBIS, p. 27; Suresh Kardi/Zuma Press p. 36; U.S. Department of Defense, News Photos, p. 39; © TRIP/D. Burrows, pp. 40–41; © TRIP/Ask Images, pp. 45, 46–47; © TRIP/W. Jacobs, pp. 51, 53; © TRIP/B. Chanjal, p. 55; © TRIP/M. Lines, p. 60; © AFP/CORBIS, pp. 49, 65; Agency for International Development, p. 61; © R. Charbonneau/ International Development Research Centre, p. 62; World Bank Photos, p. 63; www.banknotes.com, p. 68; Laura Westlund, p. 69.

Cover photo: ©TRIP/Trip